Saying Goodbye to Your Pet

Children Can Learn to Cope with Grief

Written by Marge Eaton Heegaard

To be illustrated by children

Fairview Press, Minneapolis

Published by Fairview Press, a division of Fairview Health Services, 2450 Riverside Avenue, Minneapolis, Minnesota 55454.

Library of Congress Cataloging-in-Publication Data
Heegaard, Marge Eaton.
    Saying goodbye to your pet : children can learn to cope with pet loss / written by Marge
Eaton Heegaard.
        p. cm.
    "To be illustrated by children."
    Summary: Simple text and blank spaces in which to add drawings teach children
how to cope with the loss of a pet, including how to express their grief.
    Audience: "Ages five through twelve."--P. [ ].
    ISBN 1-57749-106-8 (pbk. : alk. paper)
        1. Pet owners--Psychology--Juvenile literature. 2. Pets--Death--
Psychological aspects--Juvenile literature. 3. Bereavement--Psychological
aspects--Juvenile literature. 4. Children and animals--Juvenile literature. 5.
Children and death--Juvenile literature. [1. Pets--Death. 2. Death. 3. Grief.] I. Title.

SF411.47 .H445 2001
155.9'37--dc21   2001040701

First Printing: November 2001
Printed in the United States of America
04 03 02 01   6 5 4 3 2 1

Cover: Cover design by Laurie Ingram Duren

For a free current catalog of Fairview Press titles, please call toll-free 1-800-544-8207. Or visit our Web site at www.fairviewpress.org.

About this book

This is a book to help children (ages five through twelve) understand and express feelings of grief over the loss of a pet. Allow children to illustrate this book with pictures they choose to draw. Young children in particular find it easier to express difficult thoughts and feelings through pictures. Give them a small box of new crayons to illustrate the book, and do not make suggestions about what to draw. Some children may prefer markers, but crayons are more expressive. Older children may use colored pencils and add more words.

It is important that a parent or other caring adult be available to help children understand some of the words and concepts in this book. Try to keep children focused on thoughts and feelings rather than drawing ability.

The art process encourages communication. After every five or six pages, invite the child to tell you more about his or her pictures. Listen quietly, then share your own feelings about the loss of the pet, or talk about a pet from your childhood.

Occasionally review the completed book together so you can reminisce about the pet and reinforce important concepts learned in the text. Save the book as a childhood keepsake.

Adults can help children cope with the loss of a pet

Adults often give children a pet to teach them a sense of responsibility, but the bond between a pet and a child is stronger than many parents realize. Pets become whatever children need them to be: loving siblings, fun playmates, loyal friends. Pets offer love, comfort, and a sense of protection while teaching children to care, to give, and to trust.

Most pets live a short life, often dying suddenly of an illness or accident. Other pets get lost or stolen. In some cases, the family is forced to give their pet to another loving home: A child may develop an allergy to the pet, the family may be unable to take the pet with them when they move, or the pet may jeopardize the safety of others. (Animals can become aggressive and bite if they are afraid, provoked, mistreated, or defending their territory.) Regardless of the circumstances, the loss of a pet is traumatic. Because it is often a child's first experience with loss, the coping patterns he or she develops here are likely to continue through adulthood.

Children grieve differently than adults. They may display anger and temper tantrums, or they may cry alone in their room, uncomforted, and carry their grief silently for many years. Moreover, children frequently engage in "magical thinking" and believe they have the power to cause or prevent bad things from happening. As a result, many children feel a strong sense of guilt after losing a pet.

Children observe and learn from adults' reactions to loss, so it's important not to perpetuate mistakes adults may have made when you were a child. Children need to know it is all right to cry and express their feelings. Give them lots of hugs, as well as opportunities to develop coping and communication skills through physical and creative activities. Provide age-appropriate books to help them build a healthy foundation for future coping skills.

It is important to give children the opportunity to say goodbye to a pet. When a pet dies, do not simply discard the body. Share the facts about the loss as honestly as possible, and treat the loss with love and care. Help the children plan a ritual for burying the body or the ashes. If euthanasia is necessary, include children in the family discussion. Allow them adequate time to mourn a pet before getting a new one.

If you do give your children a new pet, choose the pet wisely. Help your children understand that identification tags, leashing, and fencing are important to help keep the pet from getting lost or stolen. Emphasize that children should never reinforce a pet's inappropriate or dangerous behavior. Finally, remind them that pets must be trained properly and treated with love.

This book is designed to teach children how to cope with the loss of a pet as well as recognize and express feelings of grief. The art process encourages communication, allowing adults to correct a child's unhealthy misconceptions and teach life-long coping skills. The text is intended to help children:

To children

This is your book. You will make it different from all other books by drawing your own thoughts and feelings. You do not need any special skills to illustrate the pages. Just use lines, shapes, and colors to draw the pictures that come into your head as you read the words on each page.

Begin with the first page and do the pages in order. Ask an adult for help with any words or pages you do not understand. When you have done a few pages, stop and share your work with an adult who cares about you.

I hope you will have fun doing this book. Sharing your problems and thoughts with others and learning some important things can help you feel better about the loss of your pet.

There are many kinds of pets.

(Draw a picture of pets that have lived with you and your family.
Add some words to tell what was special about them.)

Like all animals, pets should be loved and treated with kindness.

A pet can be very important because it . . .
(Check ✔ what you think.)

_____ loves me.

_____ makes me feel needed and important.

_____ protects me and makes me feel safe.

_____ comforts me when I am sad.

_____ never ignores me or gets angry at me.

_____ is never too busy to listen.

_____ can be like a brother, sister, or best friend.

_____ is always there when I come home.

_____ helps me learn to be responsible.

All pets are very special!

I named my pet _____.

This is a picture of me and my pet.

(Draw a picture of you and your pet.)

You are important, too!

Pets are not like toys or stuffed animals. They need special care.
(Draw some special things that pets need.)

Pets depend on people to take care of them, but people cannot always
be perfect in protecting them.

Sometimes pets get sick and need special care.

(Draw a picture of someone who helped care for your pet when it was sick.)

Veterinarians are special doctors trained to take good care of animals.

There are times when people cannot keep their pets. For example: (Check ✔ any that have happened to you.)

_____ Some people get allergies from certain pets.

_____ A pet may harm others.

_____ People may move to a place where pets are not allowed.

_____ Other:

_____ Other:

People must choose pets carefully. If they are unable to keep a pet, it's important that they try to find it a good home.

6

Even though we try to keep our pets safe, sometimes pets get lost or stolen.

(Draw a picture if this has happened to your pet, and write or draw what you think might have happened.)

It is very sad when a pet is lost or stolen.

Accidents happen. Pets can be hit by a car or killed by another animal. (Draw a picture if this happened to your pet.)

Even when people take very good care of a pet, there are some things in life that they are unable to control.

Sometimes pets get very old or sick, and no one can keep them alive—not me, not even the vet. Pets die.

(Draw a picture if this happened to your pet.)

Many pets have a short life. Dogs and cats age much faster than people do. Fifteen years is not old for people, but it is for dogs and cats.

I don't have my pet anymore.

(Draw a picture telling what happened, where, when, and why.)

It is very, very hard to lose a pet.

Sometimes when a pet is lost or stolen, it never comes back.
We might always wonder what happened, but we hope that someone
else is taking good care of our pet.

(Draw a picture of your pet in a new home.)

The time will come when you have to stop searching and hoping.
One day you will have to say goodbye. This is hard to do.

When a pet dies, its body stops working. It cannot feel anything. It cannot see, hear, breathe, eat, or play. Death is not like sleeping. No one can make the pet be alive again.

(Draw a picture of other things that die.)

Death is the natural end of living. It is very, very sad when a pet dies.

When a pet dies, the thing that made it special leaves the body. The body—or the ashes, if the body is cremated—can be buried in a special place.

(Draw a special place where a pet could be buried.)

A family may bury the body or ashes, or they might ask their vet to do it.

When a pet dies, some families have a funeral. A funeral is a special time for people to gather, share feelings, talk about why the pet was important, and say goodbye.

(Draw a picture of a pet funeral.)

This is a sad time, and it is OK to cry together.

When a pet dies, some people bury pictures or other things with their pet. Other people put flowers or a special marker on the grave in memory of the pet.

(Draw a picture of what you would do.)

It is time to say goodbye, with love.

It is hard, but it is very important for me to say goodbye to my pet.

(Write or draw something for your pet. Thank it for the love and time you had together. Tell why it was special, what you learned, what you will remember, and what you will miss.)

The word goodbye means "God be with you."

Losing my pet brings many different feelings. Some of these feelings may show on my face.

(Draw some feelings you have had.)

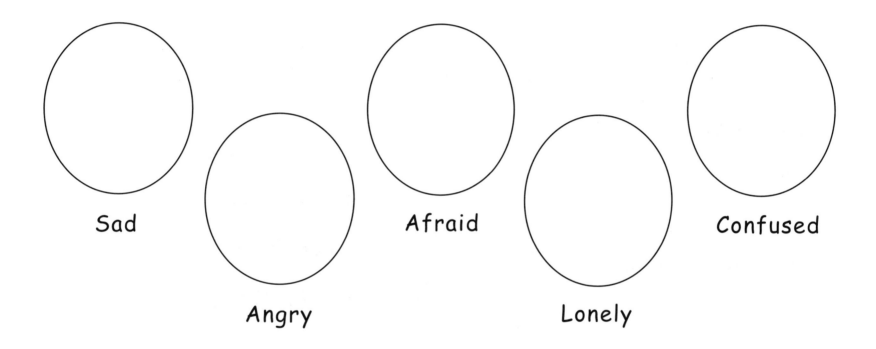

Sad

Angry

Afraid

Lonely

Confused

Some people try to hide their feelings.

(Draw a circle around any feeling you don't like others to see.)

Feelings are something I feel in my body.

(Close your eyes and think of a feeling. Color the place you feel that feeling with the colors below.)

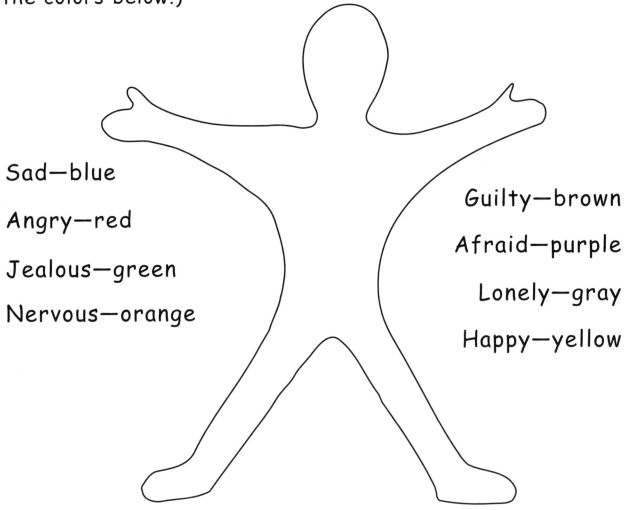

Sad—blue

Angry—red

Jealous—green

Nervous—orange

Guilty—brown

Afraid—purple

Lonely—gray

Happy—yellow

All your feelings are OK. You can learn to express them in ways that are OK.

18

Losing a pet may not feel real at first.
Some people try to pretend that it didn't happen.
The feelings that come with loss are called "grief."

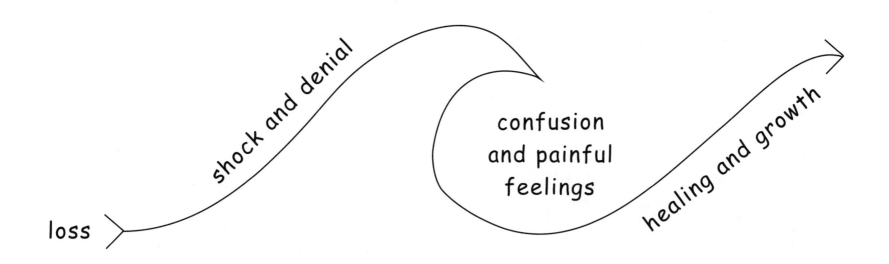

loss

shock and denial

confusion
and painful
feelings

healing and growth

Grief comes and goes like waves in the ocean.
There will be stormy times and calm times.

Some people try to avoid their grief when they lose a pet.
(Draw an X next to the things you have done.)

_____ They pretend that nothing has changed, even though things are very different now.

_____ They keep themselves busy to avoid thinking and feeling, but it doesn't change what happened.

_____ They try to replace their old pet with a new one, but each pet is special in its own way.

_____ They get angry and act mean in order to feel powerful instead of helpless, but it doesn't help.

_____ They feel guilty, thinking it's their fault, but bad things often cannot be prevented.

_____ They never get another pet so they won't risk losing it and feeling hurt again, but they lose they joy of good times.

It is very hard to lose a pet. There are things I wish I had done while my pet was with me, and there are things I wish I hadn't done.

(Draw a picture of some of these things.)

Everyone has things they wish they had done differently.
No one is perfect! It helps to talk about it and learn from your mistakes.

Everyone needs someone to talk to and share their feelings with.

(Draw a picture of someone you can talk to. Write questions you have about the loss of your pet.)

A good listener helps you let difficult feelings out.

It is OK for me to cry. Crying lets the sadness out.

(Draw a picture of when and where you cry.)

The cure for grief is called <u>mourning.</u> Mourning means expressing feelings of grief. People can comfort you when they see you mourning.

I feel angry at someone or something about what happened to my pet.
(Draw a picture about it.)

It is OK to feel angry, but it is not OK to hurt people or things.
It can help you to put your anger on paper.

There is something I fear or worry about.
(Draw a picture about it.)

Everyone has fears and worries after a loss.
It helps to put it on paper and talk to someone about it.

There are things I can do that will help me cope with my grief. I can:
(Check ✔ what you like to do.)

_____ write poems.

_____ draw or paint pictures.

_____ listen to music.

_____ play in the sand or with clay.

_____ read helpful books.

_____ do sports or other physical activities.

_____ other:

_____ other:

Sad and difficult feelings will not stay with you forever. Feelings change.

My pet was not always perfect. Nothing is!

(Draw something about your pet that was a problem.)

Most pets bring some problems with them.

I remember how I felt when I first got my pet.
(Draw a picture about that time.)

It is important to remember the good times.

I remember something funny my pet did.

(Draw a picture about it.)

It is OK to laugh and have fun, even when you are sad about something else.

I will always remember a special time with my pet.

(Draw a special time.)

It may take a while, but one day you will be able to remember the wonderful times without being sad.

30

Pets are important. Some day, when I have done my grieving,
I may want to get a new and different pet.

(Draw a picture of a new pet you might get.)

You can never replace one pet with another, but your heart is big enough to love many pets. Pets teach caring, kindness, trust, comfort, love, and responsibility, and these things will always be a part of you.

Riverhead Free Library
330 Court Street
Riverhead, N.Y. 11901
727-3228

http://river.suffolk.lib.ny.us.